My Healthy Body

Breathing

Veronica Ross

Chrysalis Children's Books

First published in the UK in 2002 by
Chrysalis Children's Books
An imprint of Chrysalis Books Group Plc
The Chrysalis Building, Bramley Road,
London W10 6SP

Paperback edition first published in 2005

ISBN 1 84138 404 6 (hb)
ISBN 1 84458 270 1 (pb)

British Library Cataloguing in Publication Data for this book is available from the British Library.

Design: Bean Bog Frag Design
Picture researcher: Terry Forshaw
Consultant: Carol Ballard

Printed in China

(T) = Top, (B) = Bottom, (L) = Left, (R) = Right.
Picture acknowledgements:
All Photography by Claire Paxton with the exception of:
4 © Bubbles/Frans Rombout; 9 (T) © Bubbles/Ian West; 10 © Digital Vision; 16 © Science Photo Library/Juergen Berger, Max Planck Institute; 24 © Corbis/Galen Rowell; 25 © Stone/Peter Cade; 26 © Ace Photo Agency/ Howard Kingsnorth; 27 © Corbis/David & Peter Turnley; 29 © Science Photo Library/Andrew Syred.

Contents

Why do I breathe?

You breathe in air to stay alive.
Air contains a gas called oxygen.
All living things
need oxygen
to stay alive.

You took
your first
breath as
soon as you
were born.

You breathe all the time without having to think about it.

You use lots of oxygen when you run and play.

Breathing in

Air goes into your body through your nose and mouth. It travels down your throat and into a tube called the windpipe. The windpipe splits into two tubes which take the air into your lungs.

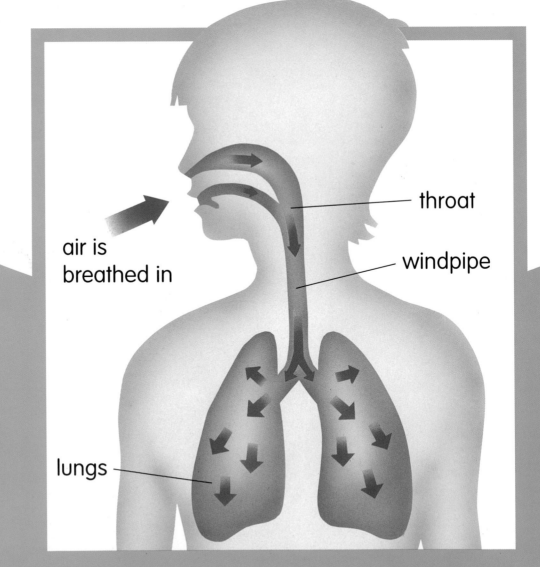

air is breathed in

throat

windpipe

lungs

In this picture you can see air entering your body as you breathe in.

Take a deep breath and blow!

When you breathe in, your chest gets bigger. This is because your lungs have filled up with air.

Breathing out

When you breathe out, stale air is squeezed up and out of your lungs and through your nose or mouth. Stale air is warm because it has been inside your body.

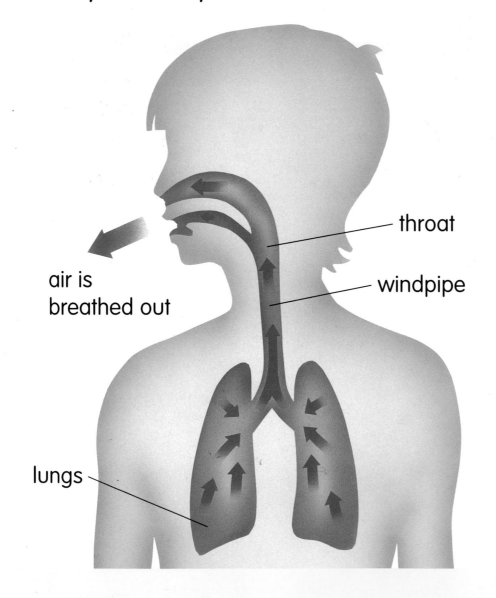

In this picture you can see the air leaving your body when you breathe out.

throat

windpipe

air is breathed out

lungs

The air you breathe out
will warm your hands
on a cold winter day.

Your chest gets
smaller when
you breathe
out. This is
because stale
air has been
squeezed out
of your body.

You can blow out
enough air to fill a
balloon in one or
two goes!

Inside your chest

Your have two lungs inside your chest. They are protected by the bones that make up your ribcage. The air that you breathe goes into your lungs.

Can you see your ribs when you stretch your arms out?

10

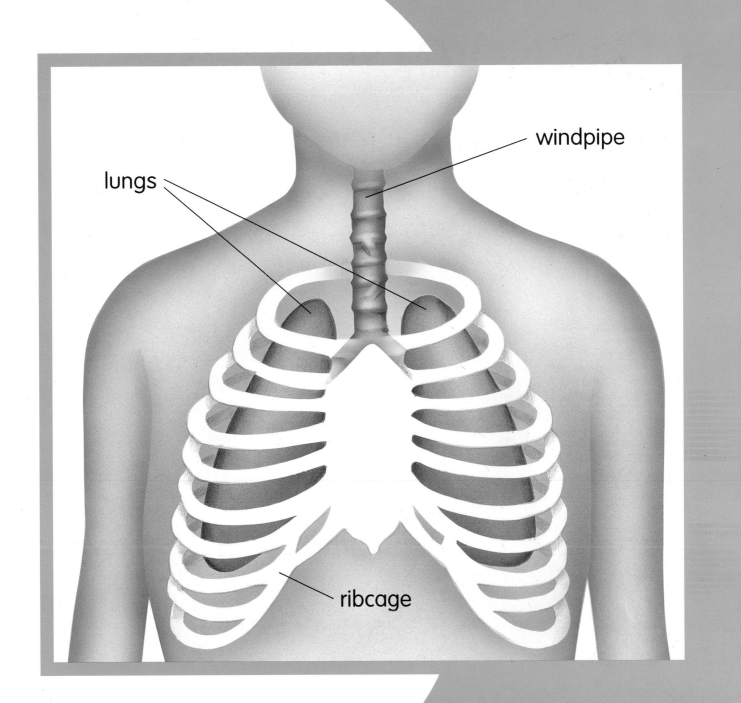

windpipe

lungs

ribcage

Your ribs move up and out when you breathe in. They move down and in when you breathe out.

Here are your lungs, windpipe and ribs inside your chest.

Your lungs

There are lots of tiny tubes inside your lungs. When you breathe air into your lungs, the air passes into these tubes and oxygen goes into your blood.

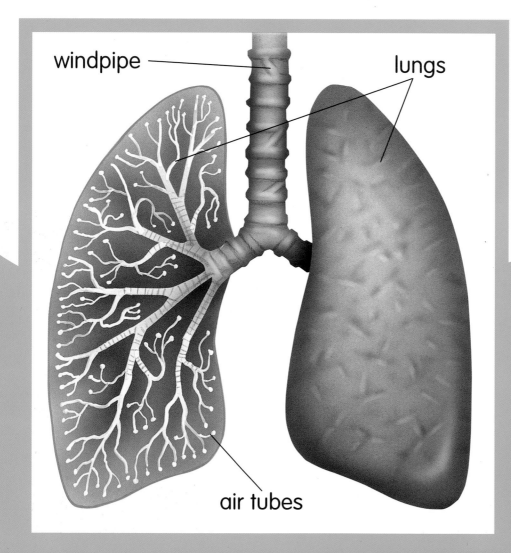

windpipe

lungs

air tubes

The narrow tubes inside your lungs look like the branches on a tree.

If you could touch your lungs, they would feel soft and squashy.

Your lungs are like two sponges. They fill with air and then empty it out.

Your heart

Your heart is a powerful muscle.
It pumps blood all around your body every
day of your life. It never stops beating.

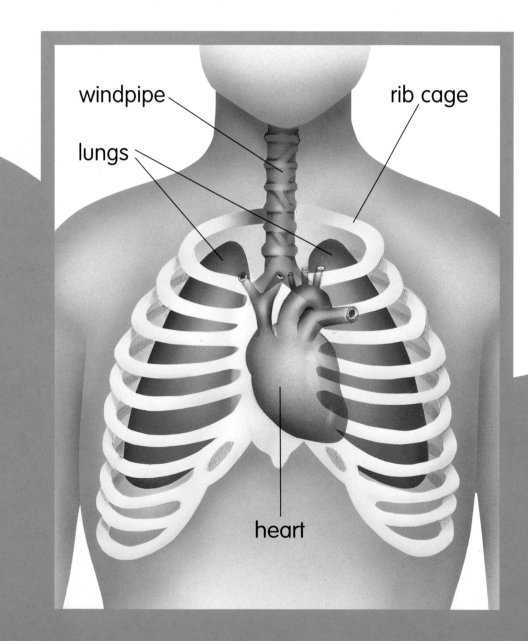

windpipe

rib cage

lungs

heart

Your heart is
between your
lungs on the
left side of
your chest.

Your fist is about the same size as your heart!

Your heart beats about 80-100 times a minute.

Can you hear your friend's heart beating?

Your blood

Blood is the red liquid that flows all around your body. It carries oxygen from your lungs to where it is needed. Blood flows around your body in tubes called blood vessels.

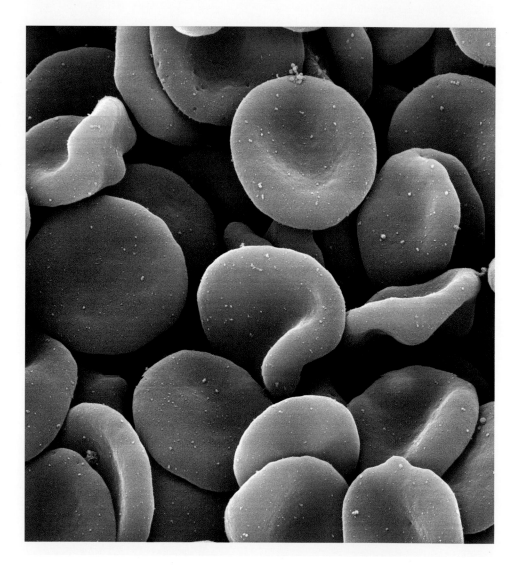

Oxygen is carried in cells called red blood cells.

Your body
contains
about three
litres of blood.

You can see
blood vessels
called veins
on the back
of your hand.

All about your nose

You breathe in mostly through your nose. Your nose warms and cleans the air before it goes into your body. There are hairs inside your nose that catch any specks of dirt.

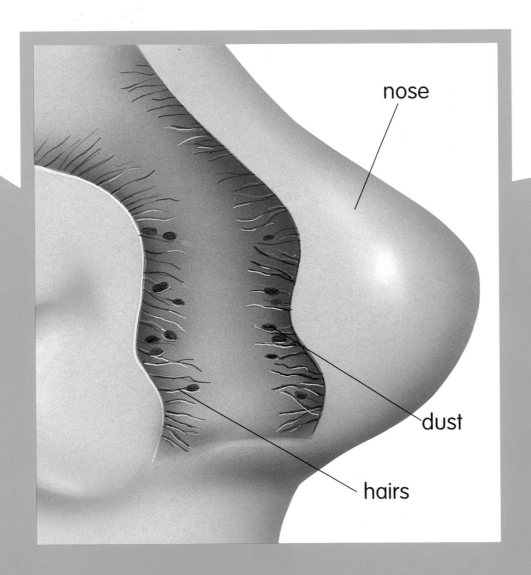

nose

dust

hairs

Any dust you breathe in is caught by the hairs inside your nose.

A sneeze
blows dirt
and dust out
of your nose.

A sneeze
can travel
at over
160 kph.

Talking

The air you breathe out is used for talking. The air goes up your windpipe and through your voice box to make sounds. You make the sounds into words using your mouth, lips, tongue, cheeks and teeth.

Look in a mirror when you are talking or singing. Your mouth forms different shapes for different sounds.

A yawn is a deep breath in and a sigh is a long breath out.

Breathing and exercise

When you are sitting still, you breathe about 12-14 times a minute. But if you have been running you breathe faster.
This is because your body needs extra oxygen to keep going.

You take about 30 breaths a minute when you have been exercising hard.

When you are asleep, you breathe slowly and your heart beat slows down.

Try counting the number of times you breathe in and out in a minute.

Something in the air

The higher up you go, the less oxygen there is in the air. This means that mountain climbers must carry tanks of oxygen with them to help them breathe properly.

This climber is using an oxygen mask to help him breathe.

We cannot breathe underwater. You must hold your breath if you swim under the surface.

There is no air in space. Astronauts must take a supply of air with them.

Pollution

The air in many towns and cities is made dirty, or polluted, by smoke from factories and by fumes from cars and lorries. Polluted air can damage your lungs and cause breathing problems.

Many cyclists wear masks to stop specks of dirt going into their lungs.

Polluted air can make you cough.
When you cough, air rushes out of
your body very fast clearing blockages
from your throat and lungs.

This factory
is pumping
fumes into the
atmosphere.

Breathing problems

Asthma is a common breathing problem. It can be caused by allergies to pollen, dust or animal mites. People with asthma can use an inhaler. This puffs medicine into the mouth and lungs to make breathing easier.

This girl is using an inhaler.

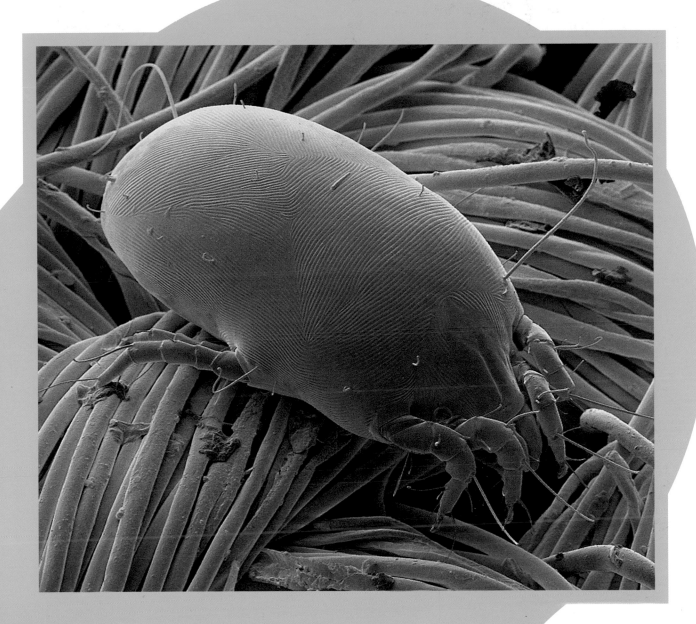

This is a dust mite under a microscope. A real dust mite is hundreds of times smaller than this one.

People who smoke cigarettes often have bad coughs and find it difficult to breathe. Smoking can cause lung disease.

Words to remember

allergy
A reaction to food or other things, such as dust or pollen.

asthma
An illness that makes people short of breath.

atmosphere
The layer of gases around the Earth.

bones
The hard parts inside your body that make up your skeleton.

cells
Tiny parts that make up your body.

dust mites
Tiny insects that live in bedclothes and carpets. We cannot see dust mites.

energy

The power you need to be able to work and play without feeling tired.

fumes

Smelly or poisonous gases that come from factories and cars.

gas

A substance that fills all the space it can. Oxygen is a gas.

lung disease

An illness that stops the lungs working properly.

muscle

Bundles of soft, stretchy fibres inside your body that make you move.

oxygen

A gas found in air.

pollen

A dust made by flowers.

ribcage

The bones in your chest that protect your heart and lungs.

Index